The Beautiful Poetry of Boris Johnson

Poetry Gem

engaging in the rendering of legal, financial, medical or professional advice.

Election night, December 12, 2019

"It does look as though this One Nation Conservative Government has been given a powerful new mandate to get Brexit done."

New Year message on Twitter, January 1, 2020

"This is going to be a fantastic year for Britain."

Announcing the signing of the Withdrawal agreement, January 24

"The signing of the Withdrawal Agreement is a fantastic moment, which finally delivers the result of the 2016 referendum and brings to an end far too many years of argument and division."

During a press conference about Coronavirus, March 3

"I was at a hospital the other night where I think there were actually a few coronavirus patients and I shook hands with everybody, you'll be pleased to know, and I continue to shake hands."

Announcing a national lockdown, March 23

"From this evening I must give the British people a very simple instruction - you must stay at home."

Revealing he had tested positive for coronavirus, March 27

"I'm working from home and self-isolating, and that's entirely the right thing to do," he said in a video message on Twitter.

On being admitted to hospital, April 6

"Last night, on the advice of my doctor, I went into hospital for some routine tests as I'm still experiencing coronavirus symptoms.

"I'm in good spirits and keeping in touch with my team, as we work together to fight this virus and keep everyone safe."

After leaving intensive care, Easter Sunday April 12

"I have today left hospital after a week in which the NHS has saved my life, no question. It's hard to find the words to express my debt. "I hope they won't mind if I mention in particular two nurses who stood by my bedside for 48 hours when things could have gone either way."

Defending his senior aide Dominic Cummings after he travelled 260 miles during a lockdown travel ban, May 24

"In every respect, he has acted responsibly, legally and with integrity."

On people returning to their workplaces after pubs and shops were permitted to reopen, July 10

"It's very important that people should be going back to work if they can now."

Pausing the post-Brexit trade talks, October 16

"The trade talks are over: the EU have effectively ended them by saying that they do not want to change their negotiating position. Only if the EU fundamentally changes its position, will it be worth talking."

Declaring a second national lockdown in England, October 31

"Now is the time to take action because there is no alternative. From Thursday, until the start of December, you must stay at home."

Revealing he would have to self-isolate after coming into contact with a Tory MP who had tested positive for coronavirus, November 16

"Hi folks, I've been instructed by our NHS Test and Trace scheme to self-isolate for two weeks, after being in contact with someone with Covid-19," he said in a video on Twitter.

"I'm in good health and have no symptoms, and will continue to lead on our response to the virus and our plans to build back better."

Promising concessions to rebel MPs before the Commons voted for tiers of coronavirus controls after the lockdown in England, December 1

"There's no question people feel that they have been unfairly attracted, by proximity, into a higher tier than they deserve," he said.

"People also feel that the tiering is not working for them."

Reacting to the UK medicines regulator approving the Pfizer/BioNTech vaccine, December 2

"We're no longer resting on the mere hope that we can return to normal next year in the spring, but rather the sure and certain knowledge that we will succeed and together reclaim our lives and all the things about our lives that we love"

“If gay marriage was OK ... then I saw no reason in principle why a union should not be consecrated between three men, as well as two men; or indeed three men and a dog.”

"I dont see why people are so snooty about Channel Five. It has some respectable documentaries about the Second World War. It also devotes considerable airtime to investigations into lap-dancing, and other related and vital subjects"

www.ingramcontent.com/pod-product-compliance
Lightning Source LLC
Chambersburg PA
CBHW061455050726
47593CB00004B/1618

* 9 7 8 1 8 0 1 3 4 5 5 4 5 *